Diez Deditos
TEN LITTLE FINGERS
&
Other Play Rhymes and Action Songs from Latin America

Selected, Arranged, and Translated by
JOSÉ-LUIS OROZCO

Illustrated by
ELISA KLEVEN

PUFFIN BOOKS

Para mi papá, Fernando,
Para mi mamá, Susana,
Para mi abuelita, María Victoria,
y para todos los niños del mundo.
¡Viva la música!

Special thanks to "el maestro" Roberto Chiófalo,
Gary Soto, and Carolyn Soto
J.-L.O.

To Julie, Anne, Mavis, Marissa, Stacey, Susie, and Ashley,
with thanks for friendship and inspiration
E.K.

PUFFIN BOOKS
Published by the Penguin Group
Penguin Putnam Books for Young Readers,
345 Hudson Street, New York, New York 10014, U.S.A.
Penguin Books Ltd, 27 Wrights Lane, London W8 5TZ, England
Penguin Books Australia Ltd, Ringwood, Victoria, Australia
Penguin Books Canada Ltd, 10 Alcorn Avenue, Toronto, Ontario, Canada M4V 3B2
Penguin Books (N.Z.) Ltd, 182-190 Wairau Road, Auckland 10, New Zealand

Penguin Books Ltd, Registered Offices: Harmondsworth, Middlesex, England

First published in the United States of America by Dutton Children's Books,
a division of Penguin Books USA Inc., 1997
Published by Puffin Books, a division of Penguin Putnam Books for Young Readers, 2002

23 25 27 29 30 28 26 24

All lyrics and music arrangements copyright © José-Luis Orozco, 1997
Illustrations copyright © Elisa Kleven, 1997
Black-and-white diagrams copyright © Judy Lanfredi, 1997
All rights reserved

Puffin Books ISBN 978 0 14 230087 9

Manufactured in China

All of the songs contained in this book have been recorded by José-Luis Orozco and are available
on CD and cassette tape from Arcoiris Records, P.O. Box 7428, Berkeley, CA 94707

Preface

Centuries of children's traditions from Spanish-speaking countries are represented in this bilingual collection of finger rhymes and action songs. Many of them I learned from my mother and grandmother in Mexico City, and others from the families I lived with while traveling in Latin America and Spain as a singer with the Mexico City Children's Choir. Still other songs and rhymes are my own creations. Over the past twenty-seven years I have had a wonderful time teaching and performing them—for preschoolers, elementary-school children, teachers, parents, even newborns! I hope every soul may have fun year-round singing, clapping, dancing—and enjoying the many themes included here, such as animals, musical instruments, parts of the body, language sounds, and, of course, family and self-esteem.

¡Ay, ay, ay!	*Ay, ay, ay!*
¡Ahora es cuando chile verde¡	*It's now or never, chili pepper!*
¡Hay que darle sabor al caldo!	*Let's spice up the soup!*
Con cantos y tradiciones	*With heaps of songs old and new*
que les traigo de a montones,	*That I bring to you,*
¡Levanto mi voz al viento	*My voice rises with the wind*
para alegrar corazones¡	*To cheer your hopeful hearts.*
¡Yo soy José-Luis Orozco!	*I am José-Luis Orozco!*
¡Para servirles a ustedes!	*To guide you on this tour!*
¡Yyyyy nooos vaaaamos!	*So, my friends, o-o-off we-e-e go-o-o!!!!!*

J.-L.O.

Contents

Diez deditos · Ten Little Fingers

Sway your open hands while singing the first three lines and then close them on the fourth. Then hold up your fingers one after another, starting with the pinkie of one hand, then the ring finger, the tall man, and so on, following the numbers in the verses.

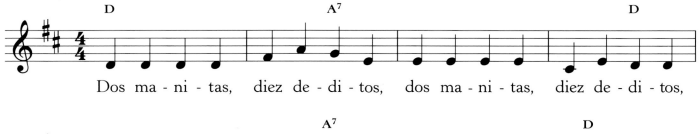

Dos ma - ni - tas,   diez de - di - tos,   dos ma - ni - tas,   diez de - di - tos,

dos ma - ni - tas,   diez de - di - tos,   cuén - ta - los con - mi - go.

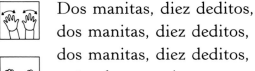

Dos manitas, diez deditos,
dos manitas, diez deditos,
dos manitas, diez deditos,
cuéntalos conmigo.

Uno, dos, tres deditos,

cuatro, cinco, seis deditos,

siete, ocho, nueve deditos,

y uno más son diez.

Two little hands, ten little fingers,
two little hands, ten little fingers,
two little hands, ten little fingers,
count them all with me.

One, two, three little fingers,

four, five, six little fingers,

seven, eight, nine little fingers,

and one more makes ten.

Tengo manita · I Have a Little Hand

This was my favorite rhyme when I was small. Before or after la merienda *(evening supper) at my* abuelita's *(grandmother's) house—which included chocolate drinks and* pan dulce *(Mexican pastry)—all the grandchildren would wait in line for a chance to sit on our grandmother's lap and have her act out this play rhyme with us. It still reminds me of those special times with her. Take the child's arm and move it gently up and down so that the child's loosely hanging hand moves up and down, too. Older children can shake their arms for themselves.*

Tengo manita,
no tengo manita,
porque la tengo
desconchabadita.

[*repetir la rima*]

I have a little hand,
I don't have a little hand,
because my little hand
is out of hand.

[*repeat the rhyme*]

San Severino • San Severino

This song, also called "San Sereni" or "San Sereni de la Buena Vida," is popular in the Spanish-speaking communities of the world. The version here comes from Puerto Rico. Clap your hands as you sing the first two lines of the song, then imitate the profession or trade mentioned in the song. Make the motions of the laundress scrubbing clothes; the tortilla maker making tortillas (since that's a clapping motion, clap here, too); the carpenter sawing wood; the secretary typing; the teacher working with children by writing on the chalkboard or saying good morning. Many other jobs/skills/trades could be added.

San Se - ve - ri - no de la bue-na, bue-na vi - da,

San Se - ve - ri - no de la bue-na, bue-na vi - da. A -

sí, a - sí, a - sí, ha - cí-a la la-van-de - ra, a -

sí, a - sí, a - sí, a - sí me gus-ta-a mí.

San Severino de la buena, buena vida,
San Severino de la buena, buena vida.
Así, así, así,
hacía **la lavandera,**
así, así, así,
así me gusta a mí.

San Severino of the happy, happy life,
San Severino of the happy, happy life.
The laundress washes the clothes.
She likes to work all day.
She likes to work all day.
I like to do it, too.

Repeat, replacing the words in boldface with the following words and phrases:

la tortillera

The tortilla maker (clap, clap, clap)

(Lyrics continued on next page)

el carpintero   *The carpenter makes tables.*

 la secretaria   *The secretary types letters.*

 la maestra   *The teacher works with children.*

¡Sí se puede! • Yes, I Can!

I dedicate this poem to all the children of the world, in love, honor, and friendship. Start with your hands above your head to show the world. Then tap your chest with both thumbs three times. Keep one hand on your chest and tap your forehead to show "intelligent." Then raise one arm above your head to show "reaching your goals." Lower it slightly, making a relaxed fist. Bring both palms to your chest, make a strong fist, and hold it to show "Yes, I can!"

 En este mundo   *In this beautiful*
tan lindo y tan grande   *and great world*

yo soy único,   *I am unique,*
yo soy especial,   *I am very special,*

lleno de amor   *and full of love.*
y de inteligencia.   *I am intelligent.*

 Yo puedo realizar   *I can reach*
mis sueños   *my goals*

 siendo un buen estudiante   *by being a good student*
y haciendo siempre mi trabajo   *and by always doing my work*

con amor,   *with love,*
con orgullo   *with pride,*
y con gusto,   *and with pleasure.*

porque sé que
 ¡sí se puede!   *Yes, I can!*

Vamos a cantar • Let's Sing

This is a song I wrote while working for several school districts in the San Francisco Bay area in the early seventies. It's a very good song for group participation. For each verse, perform or pretend to perform the action that is listed—from singing through snoring—and end with clapping.

A ho - ra va-mos a can - tar, a can - tar, a can - tar. A ho - ra

va - mos a can - tar, a can - tar, a can - tar.

Ahora vamos **a cantar**,
a cantar, **a cantar**.

[*cantar dos veces*]

Everybody **sing** *now,*
sing *now,* **sing** *now.*

[*sing twice*]

Repeat the song, each time replacing the words in boldface with one of the words below.

	a leer	*read*
	a escribir	*write*
	a comer	*eat*
	a silbar	*whistle*
	a reír	*laugh*
	a bailar	*dance*
	a saltar	*jump*
	a roncar	*snore*
	a aplaudir	*clap*

Sun, sun, ba, ba, e • Sun, Sun, ba, ba, e

I first heard this song about a beautiful bird as a small boy in Mexico, and then from a family in Pôrto Alegre, Brazil, during my childhood journeys with the Mexico City Children's Choir. Later I heard it again in Cuba. Tap the rhythm of the first two lines on your thighs. For the second two, use your hands as beaks to suggest a bird singing at dawn. Then move your hands in a zigzag for the second verse; pretend you are flying; use your hands as beaks again; jump; and pretend to go to sleep. You can also sing the verses as call-and-response, with the responders repeating the words that the caller sings.

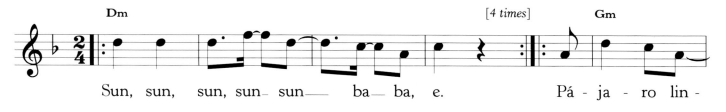

Sun, sun, sun, sun sun ba ba, e. Pá - ja - ro lin -

do de la ma - dru - gá. Pá - ja - ro lin - do, sun, sun.

Canto y respuestaj 1°: solista, 2°: todos
Call and Response 1°: solo, 2°: all

 Sun, sun, sun, sun, sun, ba, ba, e.   *Sun, sun, sun, sun, sun, ba, ba, e.*
Sun, sun, sun, sun, sun, ba, ba, e.   *Sun, sun, sun, sun, sun, ba, ba, e.*

 Pájaro lindo de la madrugá.   *Beautiful bird in the dawn of day.*
Pájaro lindo de la madrugá.   *Beautiful bird in the dawn of day.*

 Pájaro lindo, sun, sun.   *Beautiful bird, sun, sun.*
Pájaro lindo, sun, sun.   *Beautiful bird, sun, sun.*

 Vuela, vuela, sun, sun.   *Fly, fly, sun, sun.*
Vuela, vuela, sun, sun.   *Fly, fly, sun, sun.*

 Canta, canta, sun, sun.   *Sing, sing, sun, sun.*
Canta, canta, sun, sun.   *Sing, sing, sun, sun.*

 Salta, salta, sun, sun.   *Jump, jump, sun, sun.*
Salta, salta, sun, sun.   *Jump, jump, sun, sun.*

 Duerme, duerme, sun, sun.   *Go to sleep, sun, sun.*
Duerme, duerme, sun, sun.   *Go to sleep, sun, sun.*

[cantar dos veces]   *[sing twice]*

Debajo del botón · Under a Button

In this rhyme about a mouse found under a button, an adult taps his or her index finger gently on the child's chest (or button, if there is one) each time the words ton, ton or tin, tin are sung. Older children can tap for themselves. For variation, clap the hands on ton, ton or tin, tin, or tap without singing. For even more variety, clap on every syllable of the song. After a few times, you may want to leave out some words and clap them instead.

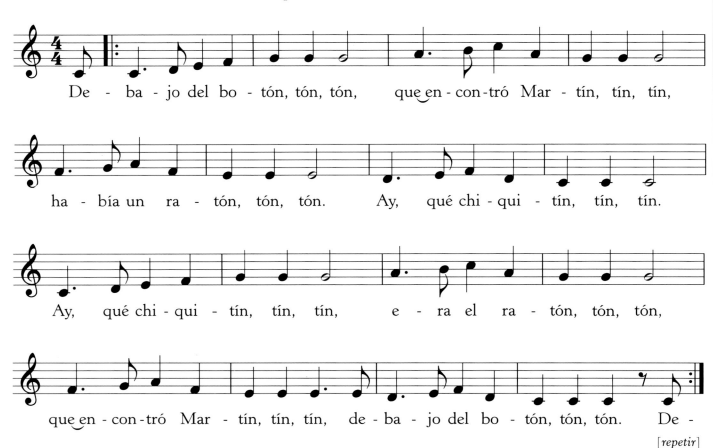

De - ba - jo del bo - tón, tón, tón,   que en - con - tró Mar - tín, tín, tín,

ha - bía un ra - tón, tón, tón.   Ay,   qué chi - qui - tín, tín, tín.

Ay,   qué chi - qui - tín, tín, tín,   e - ra el ra - tón, tón, tón,

que en - con - tró Mar - tín, tín, tín,   de - ba - jo del bo - tón, tón, tón.   De -

[repetir]

Debajo del botón, tón, tón,
que encontró Martín, tín, tín,
había un ratón, tón, tón.
Ay, qué chiquitín, tín, tín.

Under a button, ton, ton, ton,
found by Uncle Martin, tin,
there was mouse Patón, ton, ton,
playing tin, tin, tin, tin, tin.

Ay, qué chiquitín, tín, tín,
era el ratón, tón, tón,
que encontró Martín, tín, tín,
debajo del botón, tón, tón.

Playing tin, tin, tin, tin, tin,
there was mouse Patón, ton, ton,
found by Uncle Martin, tin,
under a button, ton, ton, ton.

Una rata vieja · Pancha, the Old Rat

This is an old, old song, just like the old, old rat in the song. Sing this and act it out. Make a wrinkled face to show the old rat; pretend you are ironing; pretend that you burned your tail (make an "ouch!" face); apply ointment to your hand; wrap a cloth around it; and then show what is left of the poor rat's tail by bringing your thumb and index finger close together.

U - na ra - ta vie - ja, que e - ra plan - cha - do - ra,

por plan - char su fal - da ¡se que - mó la co - la!

 Una rata vieja,

Pancha, the old rat,

 que era planchadora,
por planchar su falda

was ironing one day,
and when she pressed her skirt,

 ¡se quemó la cola!

she burned her tail away!

 Se puso pomada.

She applied some ointment.

 Se amarró un trapito.

She wrapped it in a veil,

 Y a la pobre rata
le quedó un rabito.

but the poor old Pancha,
she lost most of her tail.

Pimpón · Pimpón

I learned this song from my grandmother Doña María Victoria Ramos de Orozco, who learned it in Jalisco, Mexico. Children in Spanish-speaking countries know it very well. In a circle, sing the words and act them out. Hold up your hands to show Pimpón's hands. Pretend you are washing your face, your hands, combing your hair, wiping away tears, and shaking hands. Open and close your fingers to show the twinkling stars. Make a pillow of your hands, "Good night."

Pim - pón es un mu - ñe - co con ma - nos de car - tón. Se

la - va la ca - ri - ta con a - gua y con ja - bón.

Pimpón es un muñeco
con manos de cartón.
Se lava la carita
con agua y con jabón.

*Pimpón is a nice puppet
with hands made out of paper.
He likes to wash his face
with soap and lots of water.*

Pimpón es un muñeco
con manos de cartón.
Se lava las manitas
con agua y con jabón.

*Pimpón is a nice puppet
with hands made out of paper.
He likes to wash his hands
with soap and lots of water.*

Se desenreda el pelo
con peine de marfil.
Y aunque no le gusta,
no llora, ni hace así.

*Pimpón fixes his hair
with a comb or with a brush.
Although he doesn't like it,
he doesn't make a fuss.*

Pimpón, dame la mano
con un fuerte apretón,
que quiero ser tu amigo—
Pimpón, Pimpón, Pimpón.

*Pimpón shakes hands with me
with a big, happy smile.
He likes to be my friend—
Pimpón, Pimpón, Pimpón.*

Y cuando las estrellas
comienzan a salir,
Pimpón se va a la cama,
Pimpón se va a dormir.

*And when the stars are blinking
up in the pretty sky,
Pimpón closes his eyes,
and he whispers, "Good night."*

Juanito · Little Johnny

In this delightful song, you get to shake, jiggle, and twist different parts of your body as you sing. Clap your hands. Then in the first verse, wiggle your pinkie back and forth; in the second, shake your foot and then wiggle your pinkie. In the third verse, bend your knee up and down, then shake your foot and wiggle your pinkie. Every time you sing a new verse, add a movement until you've got your whole body in motion, from head to toe!

Jua - ni - to cuan-do bai - la, bai - la, bai - la, bai - la. Jua -

ni - to cuan-do bai - la, bai - la con el de - di - to, con el de -

di - to, i - to, i - to A - sí bai - la Jua - ni - to.

* *repetir como quiera / repeat as needed*

Juanito cuando baila,
baila, baila, baila.
Juanito cuando baila,

baila con el dedito,
con el dedito, ito, ito.

Así baila Juanito.

When little Johnny dances,
he dances, dances, dances.
When little Johnny dances,
he dances with his pinkie,
with his pinkie, pinkie, pinkie.

That's how little Johnny dances.

Juanito cuando baila,
baila, baila, baila.
Juanito cuando baila,
baila con el pie,
con el pie, pie, pie,

con el dedito, ito, ito.

Así baila Juanito.

When little Johnny dances,
he dances, dances, dances.
When little Johnny dances,
he dances with his foot,
with his foot, foot, foot,

with his pinkie, pinkie, pinkie.

That's how little Johnny dances.

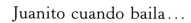

Juanito cuando baila…		*When little Johnny dances…*
la rodilla, dilla, dilla…		*knee…*
la cadera, dera, dera…		*hip…*
la mano, mano, mano…		*hand…*
el codo, codo, codo…		*elbow…*
el hombro, hombro, hombro…		*shoulder…*
la cabeza, eza, eza…		*head…*

La Pulga · The Flea Market
de San José   of San Jose

The colorful flea market of San Jose, California, reminds me of many beautiful marketplaces in Latin America. In 1971, I recorded this joyful traditional song, which I had learned as "La feria de Atitlán," on a childhood trip through Guatemala. In Puerto Rico and Mexico, the song is also known as "La feria de San Juan." Clap on the chorus, then pretend you are playing the guitar, clarinet, violin, cello, and drum. As you imitate in Spanish the sounds of the musical instruments, you will be making the sounds of the five Spanish vowels.

* repetir con los demás instrumentos / repeat this section with the other instruments

En la Pulga de San José
yo compré una guitarra,
tarra, tarra, tarra, la guitarra.

CORO

Vaya usted, vaya usted
a la Pulga de San José.

[cantar dos veces]

In the Flea Market of San Jose
I bought a guitar,
tarra, tarra, tarra, the guitar.

CHORUS

You can go, you can go
to the Flea Market of San Jose.

[sing twice]

(Lyrics continued on next page)

En la Pulga de San José
yo compré un clarinete,
nete, nete, nete, el clarinete,
tarra, tarra, tarra, la guitarra.

Vaya usted...

En la Pulga de San José
yo compré un violín,
lín, lín, el violín,
nete, nete, nete, el clarinete,
tarra, tarra, tarra, la guitarra.

Vaya usted...

En la Pulga de San José
yo compré un violón,
lón, lón, el violón,
lín, lín, el violín,
nete, nete, nete, el clarinete,
tarra, tarra, tarra, la guitarra.

Vaya usted...

En la Pulga de San José
yo compré un tumtum,
tum, tum, el tumtum,
lón, lón, el violón,
lín, lín, el violín,
nete, nete, nete, el clarinete,
tarra, tarra, tarra, la guitarra.

In the Flea Market of San Jose
I bought a clarinet,
net, net, net, the clarinet,
tarra, tarra, tarra, the guitar.

You can go...

In the Flea Market of San Jose
I bought a violin,
lin, lin, the violin,
net, net, net, the clarinet,
tarra, tarra, tarra, the guitar.

You can go...

In the Flea Market of San Jose
I bought a cello,
low, low, the cello,
lin, lin, the violin,
net, net, net, the clarinet,
tarra, tarra, tarra, the guitar.

You can go...

In the Flea Market of San Jose
I bought a drum,
tum, tum, the tum-tum,
low, low, the cello,
lin, lin, the violin,
net, net, net, the clarinet,
tarra, tarra, tarra, the guitar.

Mi familia • My Family

This little verse for the fingers is well known all over Latin America. Children can point to their own fingers, starting with the thumb and ending with the baby finger, or an adult can touch each finger of the child's hand in turn.

 Este chiquito es mi hermanito.　　　*This tiny one is my little brother.*

 Esta es mi mamá.　　　*This one is my mother.*

 Este altito es mi papá.　　　*This tall one is my father.*

 Esta es mi hermana.　　　*This one is my sister.*

 Y éste(a) chiquito(a) y bonito(a) soy yo.　　　*And this little and pretty one is me.*

Este chiquito • This One Is Little
y bonito　　　and Pretty

This starts with the baby finger and moves over to the thumb. The verse can be recited to a small child, touching his or her fingers in turn. Or kids can say it themselves and point to their fingers.

 Este chiquito y bonito.　　　*This one is little and pretty.*

 Este, señor de anillitos.　　　*This one is Mr. Ring Man.*

 Este, tonto loco.　　　*This one is Mr. Tall Man.*

 Este se va a la escuela/lame cazuelas.　　　*This one goes to school/licks the pots.*

 Y éste se lo come todo.　　　*And this one eats everything.*

Cuando vayas al mercado · When You Go to the Marketplace

This is a favorite tickling rhyme of children. The child sits on the lap of an adult or older brother or sister who recites the rhyme. The adult moves a hand in a chopping motion up the child's body, first chopping right above the knee, then the thigh, the chest or upper arm, and arriving at the shoulder. At the end of the song, the adult tickles the child's ribs or neck. Older children can act out the hand motions themselves.

Cuando vayas al mercado,
no compres carne de aquí,

When you go to the marketplace,
don't buy meat from here

ni de aquí,

nor here

ni de aquí,

nor here

ni de aquí.

nor here.

Sólo de aquí.

Only from here.

[repetir la rima varias veces]

[repeat the verse several times]

Tortillitas · Corn Tortillas

Corn and flour tortillas are a staple food in many Latin American countries. Tostadas, tacos, nachos, and chips are made from corn tortillas. Burritos, chimichangas, and sopapillas are made from flour tortillas. For this clapping rhyme, the adult holds the child's wrists and helps the child clap while reciting the words. Older children can clap and sing for themselves, alone or in a circle.

Tortillitas de manteca
pa' mamá que está contenta.
Tortillitas de salvado
pa' papá que está enojado.

Corn tortillas, corn tortillas,
corn tortillas for my mommy.
Flour tortillas, flour tortillas,
flour tortillas for my daddy.

[repetir la rima]

[repeat the verse]

Este compró · This One Bought
un huevito   a Little Egg

Starting with the baby finger, touch each finger of one hand as you say the rhyme.

 Este compró un huevito.

This one bought a little egg.

 Este encendió el fuego.

This one lit the fire.

 Este trajo la sal.

This one brought the salt.

 Este lo guisó.

This one was the cook.

 Y este pícaro gordo ¡se lo comió!

And this chubby, chubby one ate it all up!

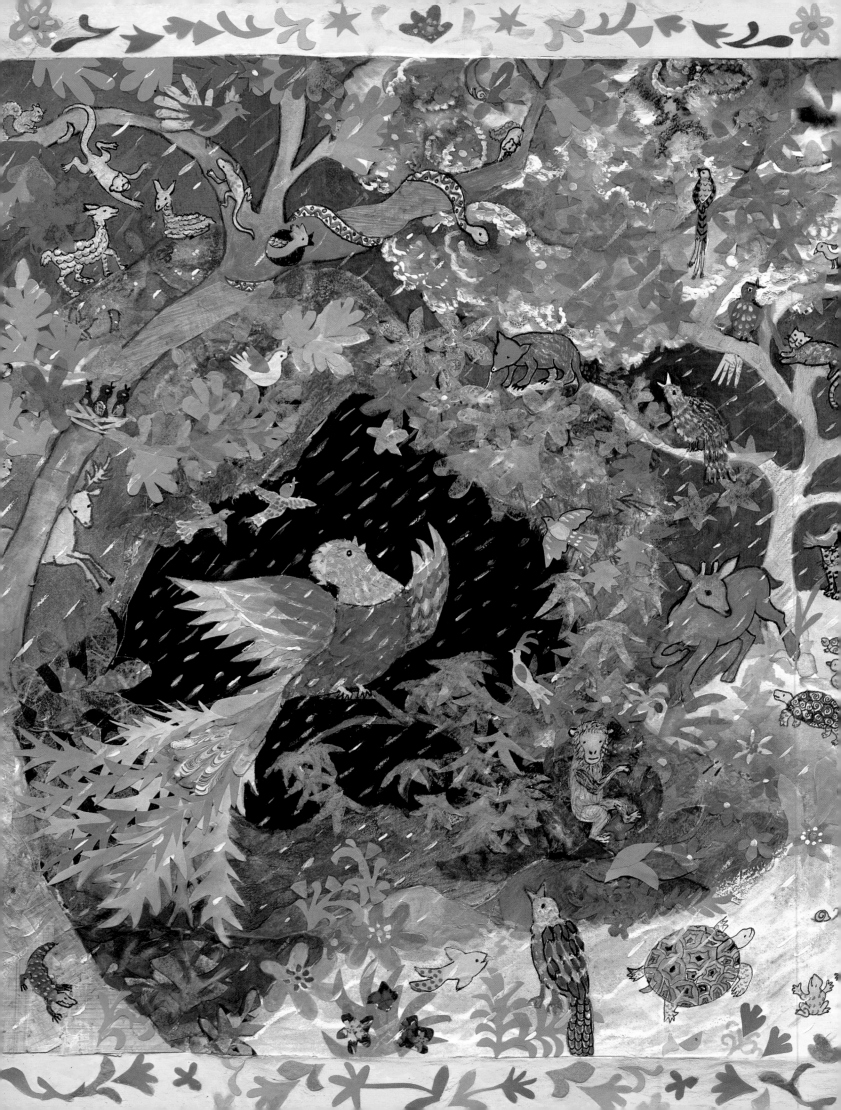

Que llueva · Bring the Rain

This song from Spain is sung throughout the Spanish-speaking world. You can imitate the rain falling by raising your arms, then wiggling your fingers as you lower them. To act out the quetzal, pretend your arms are wings. Open and close your hands to show birds twittering, and raise your arms, palms up, to show clouds rising. Act out the other animals as you like. Four are from the rain forest: the quetzal, the turtle, the deer, and the snake. Two are from the Andes: the condor and the llama.

Que llue - va, que llue - va, el quet - zal es - tá en la cue - va. Que cue - va. Los pa - ja - ri - tos can - tan, las nu - bes se le - van - tan. Que sí, que no, que cai - ga un cha - pa - rrón. Que rrón.

 Que llueva, que llueva,   *Bring the rain, bring the rain,*

 el quetzal está en la cueva. [*cantar dos veces*]   ***the quetzal** is in the cave.* [*sing twice*]

 Los pajaritos cantan,   *The little birds are singing,*

 las nubes se levantan.   *the clouds are now rising.*

Que sí, que no,   *Oh yes! Oh no!*

 que caiga un chaparrón. [*cantar dos veces*]   *Please bring us a big storm.* [*sing twice*]

(Lyrics continued on next page)

Replace the words in boldface with one of the following:

el cóndor	*the condor*
la llama	*the llama*
la tortuga	*the turtle*
el venado	*the deer*
la serpiente	*the snake*

Mi gallo • My Rooster

This traditional song is sung in many Latin American countries. Have fun with this in a circle! Cross your arms over your head to indicate a rooster; clap your hands flat to show the rooster dying; show "yesterday" with your thumb pointing backward; make a sad face and move your pointer fingers right and left to show "no more"; and move your hands as beaks for the singing sounds.

Mi ga-llo se mu - rió a - yer.   Ya no can-ta-rá co-co - rí, co-co-rá.

Ya no can-ta-rá co-co - rí, co-co-rá,   co-co-rí, co-rí, co-co - rí, co - rá.

	Mi gallo	*My rooster*
	se murió	*died*
	ayer. [*cantar dos veces*]	*yesterday.* [*sing twice*]
	Ya no cantará	*He will sing no more*
	cocorí, cocorá.	*cocorí, cocorá.*
	Ya no cantará	*He will sing no more*
	cocorí, cocorá, cocorí, corí, cocorí, corá, cocorí, corí, cocorí, corá.	*cocorí, cocorá,* *cocorí, corí, cocorí, corá,* *cocorí, corí, cocorí, corá.*

La casa de Peña • Mrs. Blue Sky

This is a special song from my childhood in Mexico. My mother and grandmother sang it to me many times. I sat on their laps and listened to their lovely voices while they jiggled my leg back and forth. The adult bounces the leg by holding it under the calf and moving it gently. Older children can jiggle their own legs.

Cuan-do me voy a la ca-sa de Pe - ña, con la pa - ti - ta le ha-go la

se - ña. Me-ne a la pa - ta, pe -rro vie -jo. Me-ne a la pa - ta de co - ne - jo.

Cuando me voy
a la casa de Peña,
con la patita
le hago la seña.

Menea la pata,
perro viejo.
Menea la pata
de conejo.

[*cantar dos veces*]

*When I go visit
Mrs. Blue Sky,
moving my leg,
I always say hi!*

*Like the dog,
I jiggle and jiggle.
Like the rabbit,
I wiggle and wiggle.*

[*sing twice*]

Campana sobre campana · Christmas Bells

Christmas in Latin America is full of happiness and celebration. Children help around the house and enjoy eating chocolate, tamales, buñuelos (fritters), and the sweet cornmeal drink called atole. Christmas is also piñata time. And at church or during the days of Las Posadas, everyone sings villancicos (Christmas carols). This one is a favorite. For the first verse, pretend you are ringing bells; then draw a window in the air, and then rock a baby. In the second verse, ring bells again, pretend to sing like an angel, then point to yourself.

Cam - pa - na so - bre cam - pa - - - na, y so - bre
cam - pa - na, u - - - na. na. Be -
lén, cam - pa - nas de Be - lén, que los án - ge - les
can - tan. ¿Qué nue - vas me tra - en? Be - lén

 Campana sobre campana,
y sobre campana, una.

Christmas bells today are ringing.
Listen to the angels singing.

 Asómate a la ventana,

Through the window we all are peeking,

 verás al niño en la cuna.

and baby Jesus is sleeping.

 Belén, campanas de Belén,
que los ángeles cantan.

The bells in Bethlehem do ring.
We hear the angels sing.

 ¿Qué nuevas me traen? [cantar dos veces]

Good news today they bring. [sing twice]

31

Mi conejito • My Easter Bunny

This is an adaptation of a traditional Mexican song about a bunny, which now can be sung at Eastertime. Just act out the verses: jump; hold your fingers up like ears; pretend you are eating grass; then look for eggs!

Sal - ta, mi co - ne - ji - to. Pa - ra tus o - re - ji - tas.

Co - me tu za - ca - ti - to, mi co - ne - ji - to, mi co - ne - ji - to.

El do - min - go de Pas - cua, voy a bus - car hue - vi - tos.

¿Dón - de los es - con - dis - te, mi co - ne - ji - to, mi co - ne - ji - to?

	Salta, mi conejito.	*Jump, jump, my Easter bunny.*
	Para tus orejitas.	*Perk up your little ears.*
	Come tu zacatito,	*Eat and eat all the grass,*
	mi conejito, mi conejito.	*my Easter bunny, my Easter bunny.*
	El domingo de Pascua,	*When Easter Sunday comes,*
	voy a buscar huevitos.	*I'll look for many eggs.*
	¿Dónde los escondiste,	*Please tell me where you hid them,*
	mi conejito, mi conejito?	*my Easter bunny, my Easter bunny.*

La pata • The Duck

In Spanish, pata is the word for a female duck and also for the leg or paw of an animal. In this song, we have fun with feet—and with words. A group makes a circle; one child is the duck in the center. That child chooses a second, then both are ducks in the center. The second child chooses a third, and so on until all the children are ducks, there is no circle, and the game starts over again. The duck inside the circle hops first on the left foot, then on the right foot, and then on alternating feet. Players making the circle clap as they sing.

Es - te es el bai - le de la pa - ta. Ha - cien - do u - na
rue - da, va - mos a ju - gar. Que pa - se al cen - tro u - na
pa - ta. To - dos can - tan - do cua - rá, cua, cua.
En la pa - ta iz - quier - da, bai - la - ba u - na pa - ta. En la pa - ta iz
pa - ta. En la pa - ta de - re - cha, bai - la - ba u - na pa - ta. En la pa - ta de -
pa - ta. En las dos pa - tas, bai - la - ba u - na pa - ta. En las dos

pa - ta. Y di - cien - do cua - rá, cua, cua, a o - tra

pa - ta in vi - tó a bai - lar. Y di - cien - do cua - rá, cua,

D.S. al Coda %
Last verse to Coda ⊕

cua, a o - tra pa - ta in - vi tó a bai - lar.

Este es el baile de la pata.
Haciendo una rueda,
vamos a jugar.

This is the dance of the duck.
Making a circle,
we are ready to play.

Que pase al centro
una pata.
Todos cantando
cuará, cua, cua.

The first duck
moves to the center.
We all sing together
cuará, cua, cua.

 En la pata izquierda,
bailaba una pata. [cantar dos veces]

One duck danced, danced, and danced
on the left foot. [sing twice]

 En la pata derecha,
bailaba una pata. [cantar dos veces]

One duck danced, danced, and danced
on the right foot. [sing twice]

 En las dos patas,
bailaba una pata. [cantar dos veces]

One duck danced, danced, and danced
on two feet. [sing twice]

Y diciendo
cuará cua, cua,
a otra pata
invitó a bailar. [cantar dos veces]

And as she sang
cuará, cua, cua,
she invited another duck
to dance. [sing twice]

(Lyrics continued on next page)

 En la pata izquierda,
bailaban dos patas.... [*cantar dos veces*]

...Tres patas
...Cuatro patas
...Cinco patas
...Todas las patas

Y diciendo
cuará cua, cua,
este baile
volvieron a empezar. [*cantar dos veces*]

Este es el baile de la pata....

Two ducks danced, danced, and
danced on the left foot. [*sing twice*]

Three ducks...
Four ducks...
Five ducks...
All the ducks...

And while singing
cuará, cua, cua,
the duck dance
started all over again. [*sing twice*]

This is the dance of the duck....

Cinco pollitos · Five Little Chickies

Hold your hand open, then close your thumb, then your pointer, and then close the other three fingers all at once. An adult can manipulate a baby's hand to play this rhyme.

 Cinco pollitos
tiene mi tía.

 Uno le canta,

 otro le pía.

 Y tres le tocan
la sinfonía.

Five little chickies
has my aunt Tamba.

One sings so pretty,

one says, "¡Caramba!"

And the three others
play a great samba!

La tía Mónica • My Aunt Monica

This song, popular in Mexico, Chile, and the American Southwest, is a great one for getting all the parts of the body moving. Clap your hands for the first three lines of the chorus, then wave them high in the air for "Ooh, la, la." For the verses, move the part of the body named, followed by a full turn around. If you get dizzy, just sing without spinning! A group can sing this in a circle, with one child being Aunt Monica in the center for one verse, and then another child for the next verse, and so on.

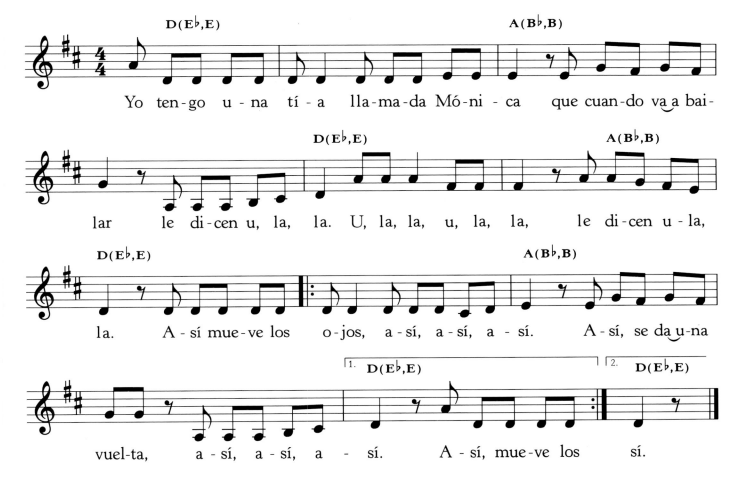

Yo ten-go u-na tí-a lla-ma-da Mó-ni-ca que cuan-do va a bai-lar le di-cen u, la, la. U, la, la, u, la, la, le di-cen u-la, la. A-sí mue-ve los o-jos, a-sí, a-sí, a-sí. A-sí, se da u-na vuel-ta, a-sí, a-sí, a-sí. A-sí, mue-ve los sí.

CORO	CHORUS
Yo tengo una tía llamada Mónica que cuando va a bailar le dicen u, la, la. U, la, la, u, la, la, le dicen u, la, la.	*I have an aunt who dances.* *Her name is Monica,* *and when she starts to dance,* *everyone goes ooh, la, la.* *Ooh, la, la, ooh, la, la,* *everyone goes ooh, la, la.*
Así mueve los ojos, así, así, así. Así se da una vuelta, así, así, así.	**She likes to move her eyes.** *She likes it just like me.* *She likes to spin and spin* *round and round like me.*

(Lyrics continued on next page)

Repeat the song, replacing the line in boldface with one of the following lines.

 Así mueve las cejas.   *She likes to move her eyebrows.*

 Así mueve las pestañas.   *She likes to move her eyelashes.*

 Así mueve la nariz.   *She likes to move her nose.*

 Así mueve la cabeza.   *She likes to move her head.*

 Así mueve los hombros.   *She likes to move her shoulders.*

 Así mueve los codos.   *She likes to move her elbows.*

 Así mueve las manos.   *She likes to move her hands.*

 Así mueve las caderas.   *She likes to move her hips.*

 Así mueve la rodillas.   *She likes to move her knees.*

 Así mueve los pies.   *She likes to move her feet.*

Así mueve todo el cuerpo.   *She likes to move her body.*

You can also add other parts of the body or substitute another name for Monica. If you want to use the name of a boy, you have to sing "Yo tengo **un tío** *llamado": "I have* **an uncle** *who dances."*

Aserrín, aserrán · Aserrín, Aserrán

This song is meant to be sung when a child is seated on an adult's lap. The adult holds the child's hands, and they both gently rock back and forth for most of the song. Toward the end, the child is pulled closer and closer so that the adult can tickle the child's throat (while still holding hands) for the last two lines.

A - se - rrín, a - se - rrán, los ma - de - ros de San Juan. Pi - den

pan, no les dan; pi - den que - so, les dan un hue - so. Se les a - to - ra en el pes-

cue - zo, y co - mien - zan a llo - rar en la puer - ta del za - guán, y les

ha - cen ri - qui, ri - qui, ri - qui, ri - qui, ri - qui, ran.——

Aserrín, aserrán,
los maderos de San Juan
piden pan, no les dan,
piden queso, les dan un hueso.
Se les atora en el pescuezo,
y comienzan a llorar
en la puerta del zaguán,

y les hacen riqui, riqui,
riqui, riqui, riqui, ran.

"Aserrín, aserrán,"
sing the termites from San Juan.
They ask for bread, which they don't get.
They ask for cheese—they get a piece.
They say, "Oh, heck! Cheese stuck in the neck!"
They all lament, and they all cry.
They sit to implore, close to the door.
Then they giggle with the tickle.
Tickle, tickle, tickle, giggle.

Las horas • The Hours

In this play rhyme, you use your arms to become a clock! Gently tip the upper part of your body from side to side, like a clock pendulum, singing the first verse twice. Then, beginning with both arms held up high at twelve o'clock, leave the right hand up and slowly move the left hand through the hours, following the song. You can go all the way around with the left arm. Or you can switch at six o'clock, and move the right arm around for the hours seven until twelve, keeping the left up high. You can also make up actions for the other verses.

Tic, tac, tic, tac. Yo soy el Se - ñor Re - loj.

Tic, tac, tic, tac. Do - ce ho - ras to - co yo.

A la u - na, co - mo tu - na. A las to - se.

CORO

Tic, tac, tic, tac.
Yo soy el Señor Reloj.
Tic, tac, tic, tac.
Doce horas toco yo.

[cantar dos veces]

CHORUS

Tick, tock, tick, tock.
I'm the clock that works all day.
Tick, tock, tick, tock.
Every hour I ring my bell.

[sing twice]

 A la una, como tuna.

Ring one, I eat with Juan.

 A las dos, como arroz.

Ring two, I tie my shoe.

 A las tres, todo al revés.

Ring three, I climb a tree.

 A las cuatro, voy al teatro.

Ring four, I open the door.

 A las cinco, pego un brinco.

Ring five, I just arrived.

A las seis, aprendo inglés.

Ring six, I pick up sticks.

 A las siete, un juguete.

Ring seven, I go to heaven.

 A las ocho, un bizcocho.

Ring eight, I watch the gate.

 A las nueve, nadie se mueve.

Ring nine, don't tickle my spine.

 A las diez, con los pies.

Ring ten, give me a pen.

 A las once, campanas de bronce.

Ring eleven, I ring up to heaven.

 A las doce, alguien tose.

Ring twelve, I see an elf.

 Tic, tac, tic, tac...

Tick, tock, tick, tock...

La raspa • Mexican Dance

There are no words in this traditional Mexican song, but plenty of dancing! "La raspa" is great fun for any special occasion. First, get a partner. Then, standing opposite your partner, hold hands, jump up, and place one heel on the ground in front of you; jump again and change feet. After every "la la la la la la" you sing, clap your hands. For the second part of the song, link right arms with your partner and swing each other around. Then link left arms and swing. Repeat this as many times as you like. This song can also be danced in a circle. Everybody in the circle holds hands and sings as they jump and place one heel on the ground in front of them, and then the other. Keep holding hands for the second half of the song while the whole circle moves to the right and then to the left. If you wish, you can make up your own words to "La raspa."

La la la la la la   la la la la la la la—— la la la la la

la   la la la la la la la—— la la la la la la   la

la la la la la la—— la la la la la la   la la la la la la la   la la

la la la la la la   la la la la la la la la   la la la la la la la

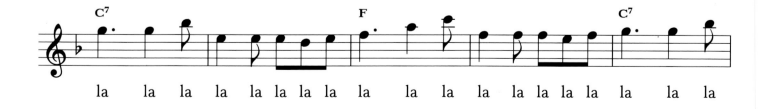

la   la la la la la la la la la   la la la la la la la la la la la   la la

la la la la la la la la la la la la la la la la la la la la la la la la la la

la —— la

Las ruedas del camión • The Wheels on the Bus

This well-loved song is perfect to sing while riding on the bus. But you don't have to be on a bus to enjoy it—just use your imagination and act out the different sounds and movements of the bus. Twirl your hands to make the wheels go, jerk your thumb when the bus driver speaks, and jiggle up and down to make the people go bumpety-bump. Rub your eyes with your hands like a crying baby, hold your finger to your lips like a shushing mother, open and close your hands to show the doors opening and shutting, and gently move your hand up and down with thumb and pointer together, pretending you are holding a coin to pay the driver. Lastly, wave your hands back and forth like wipers going swish, swish, swish.

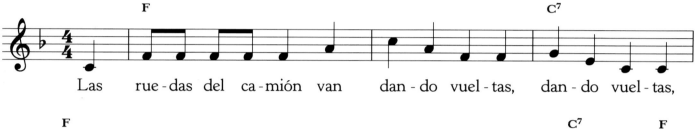

Las rue-das del ca-mión van dan-do vuel-tas, dan-do vuel-tas,

dan-do vuel-tas. Las rue-das del ca-mión van dan-do vuel-tas por la ciu-dad.

Las ruedas del camión
van dando vueltas,
dando vueltas,
dando vueltas.
Las ruedas del camión
van dando vueltas
por la ciudad.

The wheels on the bus
go round and round,
round and round,
round and round.
The wheels on the bus
go round and round
all around the town!

El chofer en el camión dice
"pasen para atrás"…

The driver on the bus
says, "Move on back!"…

La gente en el camión
salta y salta…

The people on the bus
go bumpety-bump…

El bebé en el camión
hace "ña, ña, ña"…

The baby on the bus
goes "Waaah, waaah, waaah!"…

La mamá en el camión
hace "shish, shish, shish"…

The mother on the bus
goes "Shhh, shhh, shhh!"…

(Lyrics continued on next page)

Las puertas del camión
se abren y se cierran…

*The doors on the bus
go open and shut…*

 Las monedas del camión
hacen *clinc, clinc, clinc…*

*The money on the bus
goes clink, clink, clink…*

 Los limpiadores del camión
hacen *swish, swish, swish…*

*The wipers on the bus
go swish, swish, swish…*

Tan, tan • Knock, Knock

Here your fingers are talking to one another. Hold your hands together and tap your baby fingers against each other twice, then do the same with the thumbs, ring fingers, and pointer fingers. On the last two lines, take your middle fingers and cross them left-right, then right-left, two or three times, as if they are saluting each other.

 Tan, tan.

Knock, knock.

 ¿Quién és?

Who's there?

 Soy yo.

It's me.

 Voy a abrir.

Come in.

 Hola, amiguito(a).

Hello, my friend.

¿Cómo estás?

How are you?

This finger rhyme is sung to the tune of "Frère Jacques." Start by hiding both hands behind your back for the first two lines. Bring your right hand out with thumb up, then bring the other thumb out. Next, pretend your thumbs are talking to each other, bending first the right thumb four times, then the left. For the last two lines, hide one hand behind your back, then the other.

Pul - gar - ci - to, ¿dón - de es - tá - as? ¡A - quí es - toy! ¡A - quí es -

toy! ¿Có-mo es tá us - te - ed? ¡Mu uy bie en, gra - cias! Ya me voy. Ya me voy.

 Pulgarcito,   *Where is Thumbkin?*
¿dónde estás?   *Where is Thumbkin?*

 ¡Aquí estoy!   *Here I am.*

 ¡Aquí estoy!   *Here I am.*

 ¿Cómo está usted?   *How are you today, sir?*

 ¡Muy bien, gracias!   *Very well, I thank you.*

 Ya me voy. (Adiós.)   *Good-bye.*

Ya me voy. (Adiós.)   *Good-bye.*

Continue the song for the rest of your fingers:

Señor Indice   *Pointer (forefinger)*
Señor Medio   *Tall Man (middle finger)*
Señor Anular   *Ring Man (fourth finger)*
Señor Meñique   *Pinkie (baby finger)*

49

En nuestra Tierra tan linda • On Our Beautiful Planet Earth

This is a simple song to sing in praise of our planet. You will enjoy acting out the elements of nature—the sun, moon, wind, rain, and stars. I like to sing this wherever I go. Make a big circle above your head to represent the Earth and then raise your rounded arms to show the sun. Make a small circle with your hands for the moon. Swing your arms to show the wind. Move your hands down for the rain. Open and close your fingers for the star.

En nues - tra Tie - rra tan lin - da———— pron - to va a

sa - lir el sol,———— pron - to va a sa - lir el

sol———— en nues - tra Tie - rra tan lin - da.————

 En nuestra Tierra tan linda   *On our beautiful planet Earth*

 pronto va a salir el sol,   ***the sun is about to shine,***
pronto va a salir el sol   ***the sun is about to shine***

 en nuestra Tierra tan linda.   *on our beautiful planet Earth.*

Repeat the song, each time replacing the lines in boldface with one of the lines below.

 pronto va a salir la luna   *the moon is about to shine*

 pronto va a soplar el viento   *the wind is about to blow*

 pronto va a caer la lluvia   *the rain is about to fall*

 pronto brillará una estrella   *one star is about to twinkle*

Cohetes • Fireworks

This is a hand-play piece to celebrate special occasions, like the end of a school week or a birthday, holiday, or graduation. I always use it to end my concerts because everybody likes it—children, parents, and teachers! You don't need real fireworks for it—you create your own through the sounds and actions you make. Clap your hands three times, then cup your right hand and move it upward while making a "shhh" sound. Clap three times again and then move your hand downward while saying "shhh." Repeat these gestures again, only now move your hand toward the left, then toward the right. For the "grand finale," clap your hands three times, once again moving your hand upward, downward, left, and right while making the "shhh" sound. Once you get the hang of this make-believe-fireworks celebration, speed up your movements, repeating each step faster and faster.

[3 claps] shhh [3 claps] shhh

[3 claps] shhh [3 claps] shhh

[3 claps] shhh shhh shhh shhh

[repeat faster each time]

De San Francisco vengo • I Come from San Francisco

When I was eleven, I traveled through Chile with the Mexico City Children's Choir and learned this song in Valparaíso, where it was called "De Valparaíso vengo." The song had been brought to this beautiful port city by immigrants from Austria and Germany. I changed it to "De San Francisco vengo" when I came to the United States and saw that beautiful American port city. For each new verse, the cuckoo sings one more cucú. Put your fingers together in the shape of a beak whenever the cuckoo sings. Throughout the rest of the song, you clap your hands and pat your thighs. Repeat the song as many times as you want, holding up the pointer when singing the words una vez (one time), two fingers when singing the words dos veces (two times), and so on.

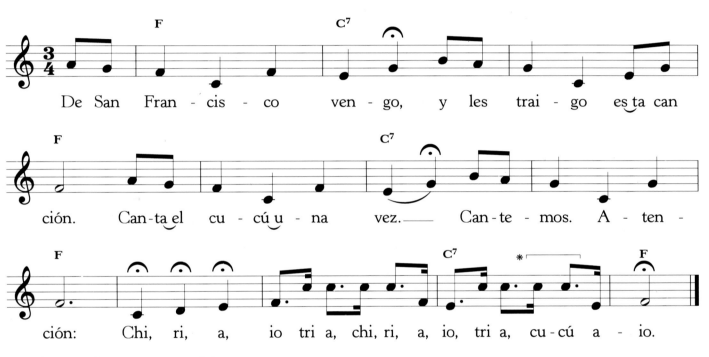

De San Fran - cis - co ven - go, y les trai - go es ta can ción. Can-ta el cu - cú u - na vez.____ Can-te - mos. A - ten - ción: Chi, ri, a, io tri a, chi, ri, a, io, tri a, cu - cú a - io.

*repetir como quiera / repeat as needed

De San Francisco vengo,
y les traigo esta canción.

*I come from San Francisco,
and I bring this song to you.*

Canta el cucú

Sing the cuckoo song

una vez.

one time.

Cantemos. Atención:

Let's all sing the cuckoo song.

CORO

CHORUS

Chi, ri, a,

Chee, ree, ah,

io

iiio,

(Lyrics continued on next page)

	tri	*tree*
	a,	*ah,*
	chi	*chee*
	ri,	*ree,*
	aio,	*iiio,*
	tri	*tree*
	a,	*ah,*
	cucú	*cuckoo*
	aio.	*io.*

De San Francisco vengo,	*I come from San Francisco,*
y les traigo esta canción.	*and I bring this song to you.*
Canta el cucú	*Sing the cuckoo song*
dos veces.	*two times.*
Cantemos. Atención:	*Let's all sing the cuckoo song.*
Chi, ri, a…	*Chee, ree, ah…*
De San Francisco vengo,	*I come from San Francisco,*
y les traigo esta canción.	*and I bring this song to you.*
Canta el cucú	*Sing the cuckoo song*
tres veces [cuatro veces…].	*three times [four times…].*
Cantemos. Atención:	*Let's all sing the cuckoo song.*
[repetir]	*[continue]*

Adiós, amigos • Good-bye, My Friends

This is a favorite call-and-response song, sung to the tune of "Frère Jacques." Wave good-bye as you sing the first four lines, tap your chest gently with both hands for lines 5 and 6, extend your arms for 7 and 8, and wave farewell again for the final four lines.

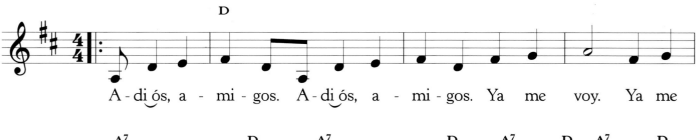

A - di ós, a - mi - gos. A - di ós, a - mi - gos. Ya me voy. Ya me

voy. Me dio mu - cho gus - to es - tar con us - te-des. A - di ós. A - di ós.

 Adiós, amigos.
Adiós, amigos.
Ya me voy.
Ya me voy.
 Me dio mucho gusto,
me dio mucho gusto
 estar con ustedes,
estar con ustedes.
 Adiós.
Adiós.
Adiós.
Adiós.

Good-bye, my friends.
Good-bye, my friends.
It's time to go.
It's time to go.
It was very nice,
it was very nice
to be with all of you,
to be with all of you.
Good-bye.
Good-bye.
Good-bye.
Good-bye.

Subject Index